Should

Black Organizations and Institutions

Be

Afrikancentered?

The Quest For Self-Determination

By

Joe Benton, LMSW

Tanya Brice, Ph.D.

Burnett Kwadwo Gallman, M.D.

Baba Derrick Jackson, Sr., Pastor

Published by Joint Ventures, Columbia, SC

First Printing March 2014
Second Printing February 2021

ISBN: 9781735974989

Note that Afrika is spelled with a "k" instead of a "c" in keeping with the spelling of most Afrikan languages in which there is no "c".

Note that Afrikan Americans are referred to as the AUSA members, the Afrikan ethnic group of Afrikan Americans. The "peculiar" institution of enslavement created one people out of dozens, if not hundreds, of ethnic groups kidnapped out of Afrika. While AUSA may have Ancestors who are Asante, Bakongo or Mende, they themselves are not Asante, Bakongo or Mende. During the almost 400 years of recent AUSA presence in the Americas, Afrikans in America have been melded into a new people, the AUSA (Afrikans from the United States of America), who have a proud heritage of resistance and creative genius.

Note that our use of the word "Afrikancentered" refers to tradition-al pre-colonial Afrika: before the Arab and European incursions.

For more information, please contact:
ImhotepTheDrum878128@gmail.com

Printed in the United States of America

About the Cover:

The symbol used is Funtumireku Denkymireku, which is an Adinkra symbol from Ghana, which means unity within diversity. It depicts two crocodiles with one stomach moving in opposite directions. Its meaning suggests that what nourishes one, nourishes the other and that they should be cooperating.

"The mission of a quality, Afri(k)an controlled, socialization process is more than a basic response to oppression. It is also a fundamental path to promote healthy individual and collective development while preventing cultural genocide."

- Asa G. Hilliard, III, Nana Baffour
Amankwatia II

Dedication

To our children, the yet unborn and those Esteemed Ancestors upon whose shoulders we stand

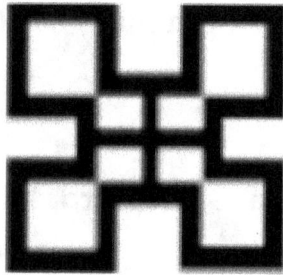

Nsaa (Excellence and Authenticity)

Acknowledgements

To those institutions and organizations that understood self-reliance as a positive means to our development and advancement as a people, such as NABSW, ASCAC, IBW, Association of Black Psychologists, Black Psychiatrists of America and others...we thank you. In addition, many thanks to Mrs. Jodi D. Gallman and Ms. Arnise N. Moultrie for bringing this project to fruition.

Aya (Defiance)

Akoma Ntonso (Agreement)

CONTENTS

Sankofa (Learn from the past)

PREFACE

Afrikan people have not only the right, but more importantly, the responsibility to tell our own story to ourselves and to the world without the oral or written permission from our oppressors. The authors of *Be Afrikancentered?* boldly argue for an ideological and cultural rupture from European thought and behavior and our internalization of many of its negative side effects in order to point the way toward cultural enlightenment and liberation, grounded in a serious narrative look at the importance of utilizing and applying orientations and knowledge derived from Afrikan history, culture, and worldviews.

The authors also highlight major contemporary Afrikancentered organizations that are committed to helping us remember what has been forgotten or ignored, while simultaneously providing knowledge and skills that demonstrate and deepen our understanding of Afrikancentered thought and behavior. One of our recent, treasured ancestors, Kimbwandende Kia Bunseki Fu- Kiau, a profound thinker on ancient African wisdom, stated in his work *Self-Healing Power and Therapy: Old Teachings from Africa* that "we are what we consume, learn, hear, see, and feel." Changing society is certainly not the same thing as changing your mind, but the authors stress the necessity for Afrikancentered thought and behavior as critical in the knowledge, debate, and dialogue in transforming both ourselves and our communities, and hence, our future.

This work serves to remind us that the collective solutions and treatments to our collective problems can and should be found within the cultural thought and practices of Afrikan people. The authors are correct to call for Pan-African alliances of parents, community organizers, and organizations at the local, national, and international level to advance this necessary cultural work. As we collectively speak and do Maat (truth, justice, and divine order) in promoting, disseminating, and integrating Afrikancentered ideas, we affirm our humanity and optimally move toward our liberation by "giving all life, power, health, stability, endurance, and joy" to ourselves, our families, and our communities.

Dr. Mario H. Beatty
International President
The Association for the Study of Classical African Civilizations (ASCAC)

INTRODUCTION

"Before Black people were stolen from Afri{k}a and brought to this country, we were culturally and spiritually alive. We were able to point to thousands of years of continuous achievements in all areas of human endeavor ranging from the scientific to the philosophical. We knew of ourselves and of our god; we were a responsible people. The institution of slavery in America was unique in that it not only demanded the physical surrender of the body; it also demanded the total surrender of the mind. Everything that made the Afri{k}an an Afri{k}an was unmercifully purged from his mind; his language, his god, his history, his art, his music, etc....The only things that were left which testified to the fact that he was an Afri{k}an were the color of his skin and the spirituality of his soul."

-Tony & Sharon Richardson, REID-C Newsletter, Vol. 2, No. 2

The enslavement, colonization, and oppression of Afrikan people by Arabs, Europeans and EuroAmericans over the past 2000 years have directly resulted in significant contemporary problems in people of Afrikan origin. This is the case no matter where in the world they are found, but especially in the USA among the AUSA.

These include:

1. Historical Misorientation, i.e., starting our history from slavery, our lowest point, and not antiquity. We have developed collective amnesia and false memories have been substituted for our true history.

2. Cultural Loss and Disunity. We have lost the desire to know our history and culture and frequently are ashamed of our culture. We frequently don't recognize when our culture is repackaged and claimed by other people.
3. Psychological Damage. We hate the way we look, and this self-hatred is frequently manifested against those who look like us. Our standard of beauty is anti-us.
4. Economic Depression and Poverty. We are consumers rather than producers and creators.
5. Health Inequities. We lead the statistics in the markers of poor health, regardless of socioeconomic classification.
6. Spiritual Confusion. We have, without question, accepted, adopted and defend the religions of those who were/are responsible for our Maafa, even when it is well documented that our Ancestors were forced into those religions for reasons of control.
7. Educational Deficits or Academic Under-achievement. Our "drop-out" rate is excessive.
8. Political Ignorance. We must hold our politicians to a higher standard than we currently do.
9. Legislative Impotence. Despite historically being the moral conscience of America, we wink at the self-aggrandizing nature of many of our politicians who "pimp" the system.
10. Legal Problems, e.g., Criminality. We don't understand the cultural and financial histories of the criminalization of our race.

11. Sexual Confusion. We have increasingly adopted the aberrant sexual practices of our kidnappers, enslavers and oppressors.

These problems are significant, and no single individual or organization can successfully eliminate them.

There are many organizations in the United States and, indeed, the world that have a "black orientation" or "theme". On the whole, these organizations are usually ineffectual and lack the needed power to affect day-to-day change and progress in the black community. These organizations are so busy trying to have a place "at the table" that they are willing to compromise what is in the best interest of the Black Community in order to maintain that place. They suffer from the "Illusion of Inclusion". Unfortunately, but as expected, their being "at the table" has not yielded the results necessary to advance the masses of Black people beyond the bottom rung of existence in America.

At the heart of this problem is the problem of "identity", which will be dealt with later. However, it can be said here that one of the most tragic aspects of this problem is that most of us don't know that we have a problem. As Dr. Marimba Ani has stated, "We are at war but only the enemy knows". The war, as our esteemed Ancestor Queen Nzinga Ratibisha Heru stated, is for the hearts and minds of Afrikan people.

Fortunately, there is a small but growing movement in the country that is finally accepting the Afrikan part of the term, "Afrikan American". Many individuals are seeking to find their Afrikan roots and it is time that the above-mentioned organizations catch that trend toward self-discovery and knowledge and provide a means toward the collective base which can speed the movement and its growth. Even more fortunate, there have been organizations that have been true to the Africanization of AUSA. Such organizations will be named, who have eschewed the "place at the 'masters' table" approach toward a more positive approach of self-determination. In effect by reclaiming our humanity on our own, developing our own institutions in all fields of endeavors and moving from their table to developing tables of our own can we change and reclaim the course of human history.

All people see the world from a position that takes into account their particular history and culture. The exception to the previous statement are the AUSA victims of the Maafa (a ki-Swahili word meaning "Great Disaster" coined by Dr. Marimba Ani to best describe what Eurocentric people call the Afrikan Holocaust). Ideally, there is tolerance and even attempts at understanding of other worldviews, but recognition of and adhering to one's own worldview is of paramount importance. It is important because one must see themselves in ways that allow them to know that they are of worth and are valued not just as individuals but also as part of a collective group that has worth and value. It is important for the health and well-being of that group that they come to know and understand the circumstances that brought them into existence. It is important for them as a group to be able to see what questions about life their group tried to answer and pass on to the next generation.

A people's sense of self-worth and self-concept comes from the knowledge (not belief) that their particular group has worth and value and also that the accumulated wisdom of their Ancestors is worthy of being studied, learned, and practiced. This is necessary in order for those yet unborn to know who they are and what their collective purpose might be. It is not enough for one to think that he or she has individual worth. It is impossible to have healthy self-worth without healthy group worth.

The exercise of people trying to separate themselves from their group creates several forms of schizophrenia. When individuals within a particular group have no knowledge, respect for or appreciation for the group to which they belong, they will seek out another group to satisfy the human appetite to belong to something greater then themselves. They will then take on the cultural identity of another group and participate in behaviors that might be dangerous to their own development. In order to produce people who are healthy and have a healthy concept about themselves we have to have organizations and institutions that have a healthy outlook about being Afrikan. In order for our institutions and organizations to be considered healthy they have to reflect the culture, history, and traditions of the people they are supposed to be serving. If the people who are the leaders and the members of these organizations and institutions do not have a healthy worldview of their own people, then they will reflect the history, culture and traditions of another group of people and then wonder why their own people are not advancing.

There are three words that we should understand:
- **Member:** a person, animal, plant that is part of a society, group or other body.
- **Dis-member:** to break the member away from itself.
- **Re-member:** through accurate memory, the member is made whole and regains a sense of membership.

In an Afrikan sense, we were born members of great Afrikan civilizations and societies. However, with the onset of colonization, enslavement, oppression, reeducation and re-socialization, we became dismembered. We were broken away from ourselves spiritually, emotionally, physically and mentally.

With no chance to remember, we could not even become part of the human race. We lost our names and were told we were less than human and we, too often, believed it. Organizations such as the National Association of Black Social Workers, the Association of Black Psychologists and the Association for the Study of Classical African Civilizations are part of the remembering process that is so desperately needed in order to restore us to our rightful place in humanity. Without such remembering, we will remain at the bottom of all that is good and at the top of all that is bad.

Almost all people who see themselves as white have a worldview that is frequently called Western Civilization. They have attempted, with some success, to universalize their worldview to the exclusion and detriment of others.

Everything from Santa Claus to religious symbols and figures are labeled as "white" and any other coloration is deemed an aberration. Many, if not most of the people that they have influenced see ancient European history, religion and culture as "classic" even though they are not European.

It is believed by many that the struggles of the past have created a level playing ground and that AUSA do not need to "separate" themselves from "society" (meaning white society). They frequently believe that just because we have a president with Afrikan origins, that we live in a "post-racial" America. This type of thinking displays an ignorance of the past and a flawed vision of the future. America has never in its 200 plus years shown any respect for Afrikans as human beings, including the "black president" and certainly has shown no appreciation for our Ancestors' contributions to world civilization and to the building and development of this country.

When will we, as a group, come to the conclusion that America will never treat us as equals on the scale of human equality unless we become upright, correct and proper through an understanding and appreciation for self? We must come to the table of humanity not as beggars waiting for the crumbs of Western society but as designers, architects, and engineers of what it means to be human. Without contact with our ancient Afrikan Ancestors, Europe would have not moved past barbarism. One cannot learn that information following a western paradigm.

In the movie *Malcolm X* , the man said "Get your hands out of my pocket" before shooting Malcolm. We have to remove our collective hands out of the pockets of Eurocentric institutions and organizations so we can have a real family discussion about what to do for the AUSA Nation. Most of our institutions and organizations currently cannot afford to be Afrikan-centered for the simple reason of whose hands are in our pockets and in whose pockets our hands are in. One cannot have the courage to voice what needs to be said if we have our collective hands in the pockets of those whom we say are oppressing us.

To paraphrase our esteemed Ancestor, Dr. Asa G. Hilliard, III, the Afrikancentered community and organizations must control the socialization of people into Afrikan culture. This is required for our survival as a people and a culture.

After the civil war ended, a group of our Ancestors were asked a question by General Sherman of the Union army. When asked what slavery meant to them, they replied, "Slavery is when another man benefits from your labor." Then when asked what freedom meant to them, they replied, "Freedom is when you benefit from the fruits of your own labor". We are still enslaved in the 21st century because we are still not collectively benefiting from the fruits of our own labor. Because of their answers, this became the origins of General Sherman's Field Order 14 known as 40 acres and a mule. It was about their definition of freedom. Their definition was simple yet elegant in its understanding of what it means to be human and free.

After the end of Reconstruction, Frederick Douglass, a prominent 19th century AUSA leader, came to the conclusion that the only way we were going to get what we needed was through self-reliance. He said, "We must not beg men to do for us what we ought to do for ourselves". Afterwards, Langston Mercer, a Howard University professor, picked up the call for self-reliance and said "The hour has come for us to manage our own institutions. If we have colored banks, we must have colored bankers; if we have colored schools, let us have our own teachers".

The ideological language of AUSA people at the end of Reconstruction was a combination of political, social, and economic rights with the ideals of self-reliance and self-determination which became the impulse for our in-stitution and organization building post reconstruction. We must recapture that same ideology today in order to save our people from the self-destruction we now see in our communities. If we don't then we are headed for extinction as a people. In order to truly understand Afrikancentered thought, one must understand the system of white supremacy; its history and its manifestations such as racism (and the corollary of racism, white privilege), sexism, ageism and classism. Understanding white supremacy goes far beyond being mired in simply understanding racism. This is a trap that many of us have fallen into.

So...the answer to the question posed in the title of this book is a resounding **"YES"**!! Read on to find out what, why and how.

Bi Nka Bi (Harmony)

WHAT HAPPENED?

In this book, we have posed a question that many have found challenging. Perhaps, this first chapter will offer explanations that resonate with you, the reader.

The authors, all being in healing and/or medical science fields wish to approach the problem as if we were approaching a patient with a disease or disorder, such as amnesia or addiction.

The first step in healing is recognition that a problem does, in fact exist. This is frequently the most difficult problem. Afrikan people throughout the world have undergone a process that resulted in the destruction or dismemberment of their self-recognition as Afrikans. In fact, many Afrikans deny that they are Afrikan, preferring to adhere to the geopolitical nationality imposed upon them as a result of enslavement and subsequent assimilation. This process was necessary to create and maintain a vanquished people who did not realize that they were vanquished. Some call it colonization of mind, body, spirit and culture. Others have called it mental slavery, mis-education and misorientation. This condition has been severe in Afrikans on the continent but especially extreme in those of us who are in the diaspora. As we have done throughout the book, we will continue to concentrate on Ausa people although the explanation is international in scope. We must, then, agree that a problem does exist. We must also agree that the factors that created, sustained and perpetuated the problem are still in effect today.

The next step in healing is establishing an etiology (cause) and pathogenesis (origin, development and resultant effects of a disease) of the problem. This requires at least a basic understanding of world history. Briefly, when Europe invaded other countries (including Afrikan countries as well as Ireland and India) for the acquisition of their land as well as their human, mineral and other resources, they recognized that it was necessary to completely subdue these people culturally and mentally as well as militarily. Why they did what they did is explained in detail by Dr. Marimba Ani in her profoundly important book, Yurugu. Suffice it to say that they saw that they had to control the education and socialization of the societies...to control the minds and thinking of their foes and to control their values. One of the first things that they did was to discourage (through force or farce) the use of the native language. This was an effective way of severely damaging the culture. They then mapped out the land and changed the names of places before changing the names of the people. They then brought in the teachers and missionaries who taught the subject peoples to be ashamed of their appearances, their belief systems, their way of speaking and anything relating to their native culture while teaching the colonized people that the colonizer's religion was superior, their culture was the standard and that their appearances were examples of true beauty. An "educated" (some call it "mis-educated") elite was frequently set up to mold and guide the rest of the people and they frequently did not understand that they were being used to further maintain the destruction of their people. If they caught on to what was happening, they were frequently killed.

Many have blamed our problems on racism/white supremacy. We propose that plain racism cannot do the damage that has been done to us, so one of the major factors affecting the lives of Ausa is structural or institutional. Race is a social construct and not a biological reality however it is a tool that has been used to justify the inhuman and horrific treatment given to Afrikan people because of our appearance. So, to paraphrase Thiongo, Afrikan consciousness is the right of Black peoples to create and adopt an image of themselves that negates and transcends the image of themselves that was created by their enemies. We must also realize that the problems we face are not just matters of race. If we removed race as the only issue, our problems would still exist. Look at the example of Ireland. They are white and were colonized and much of what happened to Afrikan countries also happened in Ireland. We need to examine other factors that may be contributing to the problems that we face and that have existed over time.

We submit that a major contributor to the problems we face is what Fanon called "Structural Oppression". Oppression is the condition of being involuntarily dominated or controlled by another person or group, so this further demonstrates that race is a tool used in oppression. Oppression is profoundly insidious because a person does not need to realize that he or she is oppressed in order to be oppressed. In fact, we feel that most Ausa do not realize that they are oppressed. In fact, Harriett Tubman is frequently credited with saying that she would have freed more slaves if they had known that they were slaves. Unfortunately, there are many people in our community who help to maintain, sustain and perpetuate their own oppression (intentionally and unintentionally).

Frequently, the oppressor uses sophisticated and complex messages to communicate to the oppressed that they are to blame for their own oppressed condition. This is called "blaming the victim". The oppressed people are taught to feel fortunate when they can be in the same room with or be tolerated by their oppressors and ecstatic when they please their oppressors. "Blaming the victim" is a proven method that can be found in almost every oppressive system. It takes a certain level of consciousness and a concerted effort at transcendence for an oppressed person to rise above the self-blame syndrome and/or to clearly understand the insidious forces at work in their oppression. This is an extremely difficult task and for too many, this clarity is never achieved.

Another method used by the oppressor is to make the oppressed feel the need to aggressively seek acceptance even though they can never be fully accepted.

Traditionally, when most people think of oppression, it is viewed from the perspective of tyrannical, dictatorial and authoritarian actions. It is equated with power, however, power does not have to be dictatorial or authoritarian.

As Dr. Wade Nobles has said, "Power is the ability to define reality and have other people respond to your definition as if it were their definition". Structural oppression uses relationships based in and on power. As a result of these power relationships, we find structures in place that produce results that become the manifestation and definition of oppression.

According to Iris Marion Young, there are five faces of oppression. They are:

1. Exploitation. This is the transfer of the rewards of labor from one social group to benefit another.
2. Marginalization. People who are expelled from useful and meaningful participation in social life.
3. Powerlessness. This describes those who lack authority or power to make decisions that affect their lives. They take orders and are rarely in a position to give orders.
4. Cultural imperialism. This occurs when the dominant group determines for all other groups what it means to be human while rendering the particular perspectives, opinions, and beliefs invisible and invalid. The dominant group establishes its experiences, history and culture as the universal norm.
5. Violence. Ausa live with the knowledge that they must fear random, unprovoked attacks on their persons and property, not only in Florida but all over the world.

For these power relationships to work, the dominant group must not only see themselves as dominant and superior, but the oppressed group adapts and internalizes their subordinate and inferior position. We then find that, as we've stated, the dominant-superior group creates strategies and techniques to perpetuate structural oppression. These (and other) techniques are frequently used to distract the oppressed people and to disguise the true problems. The "-isms" e.g., racism, sexism, ageism, classism, anti-Semitism, etc. are examples of these techniques.

It is important to realize that we find the faces of oppression in each of the nine Areas of Human Activity given to us by Dr. Frances Cress Welsing (Politics, Entertainment, Law, Labor, Economics, Religion, Sex, Education and War). Although beyond the scope of what we're doing here, it would be a useful exercise to find the structures of the faces of oppression in each of these Nine Areas of Human Activity.

Next, we have to recognize and understand the symptoms and signs of our cultural destruction, structural oppression and "mentacide" (as Dr. Bobby Wright called it). Some of these symptoms and signs are:

- Hating everything about oneself that is Afrikan (color, features, temperament) without actually realizing it.
- Being convinced that feminine beauty is long and/or straight hair, thin lips, light skin, and being skinny.

- Wishing that one was white (consciously or unconsciously).
- Trying to be accepted by and not offending white people.
- Believing that we are in a "post-racial" era and that racism is not only a thing of the past but doesn't affect them.
- Not "connecting the dots" to understand why Ausa lead in the negative statistics and lag in the positive statistics.
- Not understanding how history has contributed to our condition.
- Seeing Europe as the "classical" civilization with European artists as "masters" and European music as "classical."
- Not caring to learn anything about the history of Afrikan people because it doesn't seem important.
- Having deep feelings of inferiority to whites and trying to never offend them regardless of the fact that they are frequently offensive to us.
- Seeing Afrikan people as basically dishonest, lazy, stupid and "trifling".
- Believing that "education" and merit will cause success while not recognizing unearned racial and colonial privilege.
- Believing that anyone of Afrikan origin, including presidents, prime ministers, representatives or senators, has true power in the Western world.
- Victimizing one's own people and defending others who victimize them.
- Not admitting to being Afrikan.

- Not only not knowing one's history but being indifferent or unwilling to learn the history of one's own people.
- Having tattoos of symbols from other cultures rather than the deeply profound symbols found all over the Afrikan continent.

Once the diagnosis has been made, based on an analysis of the etiology and review of the symptoms and signs, a therapeutic approach has to be created. This is where sound reasoning has to be used. It should be realized that we will not negate the de-Afrikanization that took hundreds of years to create, in one, two or even five generations. We should understand that as long as there is clarity on the desired end result, there are at least several ways of approaching the problem. We cannot afford to get bogged down in silly disputes involving method.

Re-education is probably the major road to Re-Afrikanization. This can be done is several ways including study groups, lecture series, after school programs, Rites of Passage programs and charter schools. Adults and children are the targets, but in our experience, children tend to "get it" sooner. The question may be asked, re-education for what? There is no single or simple answer. One thing that is definite is that we have to know our history as told by our historians and scholars. As Dr. Wade Nobles has said,

"The role and purpose of education is to allow each generation in society to rationally guide and systematically guarantee that it reproduces and refines the best of itself and by so doing, pass

on to the next generation its accumulated wisdom, and the knowledge and skills necessary to develop, maintain and participate in the society of the future."

There is no easy way around this. In order to know who we are, we must know who we were. We have to respect, honor and venerate our Ancestors. Next and perhaps most importantly, we should adopt the best of our traditional culture, especially the values.

So...

Our quests, as a people, to live, love, create and develop as human beings should be the guiding aim of our organizations. The quest to fulfill the agendas of other people should not be part of our goal structure. Toward that end, the measurement of progress should not be the attainment of goals set by others but goals that we determine based on our knowledge of self. We all know that our people suffer and are found, statistically, at the bottom of life expectancy, health and wealth, which are key factors in determining happiness and well-being.

Our organizations have a clear mission in establishing goals which will not only bring about happiness and well -being of our people but will contribute toward making substantial gains in getting us off of the bottom. It is often said that rising tides lift all boats. Rising tides may well be true for boats but does not translate into human behavior or reality. In regard to wealth, the rich get richer and the poor remain poor and often only get imprisoned for their efforts. As the rich rise the poor become poorer and sink lower into the abyss. Our organizations should be setting goals, means and methods for enriching our people and organizations culturally and financially. In observing the rich it becomes increasingly clear that intelligence and wisdom are not the means of becoming rich. That means understanding the process of how wealth is obtained. Many of today's rich have inherited their wealth. However, the path to wealth in this world comes down to ownership, controlling modes of production and distributing goods and services to those who demand them. Demand is not just wanting goods and services but in economic terms means those who want and can pay for those goods and services. These individuals are called consumers. Our measure of progress then becomes how much we own, control, produce and deliver rather than how much we consume.

Another goal has to do with our health. Adult onset diabetes, high blood pressure, high cholesterol, kidney failure with dialysis, cancer and heart disease coupled with low birth weight babies, miscarriages and high infant mortality consumes our people's health dollars. STD's such as HIV and other chronic infections such as Hepatitis factor into this also. The sad part of most of this is that many of these diseases and conditions are preventable. Prenatal care, exercise, good diets, stress reduction and lifestyle discretion should be daily staples of our existence. Our organizations should have clear and concise health goals and strategies. We should not allow our children's schools to decrease physical education and the arts and music in the curricula. Our organizations should also inject overt health messages into everyday schooling. Workplaces should allow time for physical, intellectual and emotional health as part of the workday. Increased productivity in both our schools and at our jobs should be seen as an ideal rather than a fantasy.

Wealth and health are the keys to a long life. On the whole, in this society, those who are the wealthiest and the healthiest tend to live longer. Access to critical medical care, wholesome foods and sufficient leisure time and recreation decreases stress and the related illnesses attributed to stress. The lessening of stress, on the whole, will improve the quality of daily life and will ultimately move our people from the bottom.

These large-scale movements in attaining wealth, obtaining health and increasing our life expectancy can only be realized through the transformation of how we view ourselves. Organizations have to advance the idea that we are worthy and capable as human beings to thrive in this society on our own terms. We have to do this on our own, as did our ancient Ancestors. We have to demonstrate to the world that we not only have overcome but we have also flourished in incubation chambers and environments where we were supposed to perish. And we've done this on our own terms with our culture as the background. This then becomes "our table", where only we can partake and develop.

Every system in this society is but a stepping-stone on the path which our Ancestors carved. It is up to us to restore our people and our organizations to that path which could set the world on a new and better trajectory. That trajectory would be based on our value system and principles. Any people who could lift themselves up from the bottom to the top would set an example for others to follow. We must emphasize the notion that all AUSA people must prosper and achieve together for mutual benefit. Though poor in wealth, our people are not poor in resources. We lack the will and the tools to make our resources to work harmoniously for the collective good at this point in time for the reasons given above. This behavior is a direct use or misuse of what we have learned from alien (European and Arab) culture. The cult of the individual has become a plague upon people of African descent and has much to do with our languishing on the bottom of societal measures. The restoration of African culture and values should be the prime directive of all African centered organizations.

What can be done is clear and what has to be done is even clearer. Our goals and mission lie directly before us. Our lives as a people are at stake and our time cannot be wasted attending to the goals, missions, enrichment and betterment of others.

Black organizations should not only be Afrikan Centered but also Pan Afrikan.

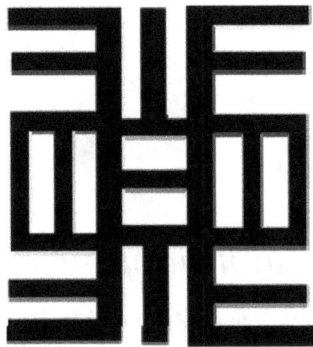

Nea Onnim No Sua A, Ohu (Knowledge, Lifelong Education)

Knowledge of our history and culture is the glue that bonds us together and gives us a sense of purpose in life.

-Jacob Carruthers

WHAT IS AFRIKANCENTERED?

Afrikancentered is seeing the world from the perspective of an Afrikan person and accepting your place in world history. It adheres to the cultural aspects of the Afrikan World view. Western education trains us to see the world from a Western (European or Eurocentric) perspective. All people should see and accept the world from a perspective consistent with their own particular history and cultural mores.

Culture is the totality of thought and practice by which a people creates itself and presents itself to history and humanity. It has been said to represent the behavior and habits of one's Ancestors. It is the beliefs, values, and attitudes of a group which affects members of that group's beliefs and attitudes. It includes:

Axiology (the governing nature of relationships). In the Eurocentric worldview, the highest value lies in the object or in acquisition of the object. In the Afrikan worldview, the highest value lies in interpersonal relationships between members.

Cosmology (the way a people see the universe). In the Eurocentric worldview humans are apart and separate from nature while Afrikans see all things in the universe as interconnected.

Epistemology (the nature of knowledge-how do we know). In the Eurocentric worldview one knows through counting and measuring. In the Afrikan worldview, one knows through symbolism and rhythm.

Aesthetics (the governing nature of beauty).

Eurocentric aesthetics are about the physical and the external while Afrikan aesthetics are about reaching ones highest potential and valuing the internal as well as the external.

Ideology (the body of ideas reflecting the social needs and aspirations of a people, the manner or content of thinking characteristic of an individual, group or culture). In the Eurocentric culture, there is a drive for mastery and control and the accumulation of possessions while Afrikans stress the oneness of all things and group maintenance. Collectiveness and sharing are essential.

Ontology (the nature of reality). The Eurocentric view measures worth by utility, therefore materialism is paramount while to Afrikans, all things have spirit and therefore, have worth.

Ethos (the fundamental values of a people). The Eurocentric dictates control and mastery of all life while to Afrikans, all things should be with and in harmony with nature.

Logic (reasoning). Eurocentric logic is dichotomous (either/or) while Afrikancentered logic is diunital or the union of opposites.

Pedagogy (teaching). Eurocentric pedagogy deals with parts that lead to the whole while Afrikancentered pedagogy is holistic and deals with the entirety.

Process (progressive course). Eurocentric process states that everything is repeatable and reproducible while the

Afrikan worldview posits that all things are interrelated through human and spiritual networks.

Methodology. Eurocentric methodology is linear and sequential while Afrikancentered methodology deals with critical path analysis.

Much of the above information comes from Edwin. J. Nichols, Ph.D. The Philosophical Aspects of Cultural Difference

History tells a people where they have been and what they have been. It also tells a people where they are and what they are. Most importantly, history tells a people where they still must go and what they still must be."

-John Henrik Clarke

TO BE AFRIKANCENTERED IS...

To be Afrikancentered is to place value on, give respect to and honor the Creator, our Afrikan Ancestors, and ourselves.

To be Afrikancentered is to see the beauty in ourselves. It is to see all our physical characteristics as beautiful and desirable. It is to accept our varied and unique physical appearances as the norm—as the standard of beauty. It is to understand dialectics (defining things by their opposites) and avoid inadvertently demeaning ourselves by using terms such as "good hair" and "she was real dark *but* pretty anyway".

To be Afrikancentered is to honor and uplift your humanity and the humanity of your Afrikan Ancestors who created civilizations, originated sciences and disciplines, attempted to share information about spirituality, and frequently sacrificed comfort and even life, for us. In honoring these Ancestors, we acknowledge the fact that we do not walk the earth alone but with the guidance of those who came before us if we would take the time and expend the effort to listen to them.

To be Afrikancentered is to accept your place in the world and world history.

To be Afrikancentered is to be a part of and accept the collective consciousness and maturity of the first humans to inhabit the earth.

J. Benton, T. Brice, B. Gallman, and D. Jackson

To be Afrikancentered is to understand that the true struggle of humanity is not a struggle for power and domination but a struggle to live in harmony with nature, with the universe and with all the Creator's creations, especially other human beings.

Gye Nyame (Except for God)

J. Benton, T. Brice, B. Gallman, and D. Jackson

To be denied historical achievement is to be placed outside of humanity, for only humans make history.

-Maulana Karenga

WHY AFRIKANCENTERED?

The fact that this question has to be asked speaks to the fact that Ausa people have been intellectually, spiritually, and psychologically victimized with information that is detrimental to their development and advancement as human beings. It says that there is something missing and wrong with Afrikan people. It should be obvious that being Afrikancentered is a necessary component for our healing and further development as human beings.

All persons of Afrikan origin need to at least know their native culture. They need to understand the historicide that has been perpetrated against them. They must know the truth about who they really are. Afrikan people need to deal with the three questions that Franz Fanon said that each Afrikan person needs to address and understand:

> Who am I?
> Am I really who I
> am? Am I all that
> I can be?

These questions deal with the Identity part of the triad that we all should consider and seek from our youth. This triad is Identity, Purpose and Direction. Identity determines purpose and direction and if our self - concept is alien to our true selves, our purpose and direction will be detrimental to our people. We cannot be Eurocentric and actually be true to ourselves and to our people. Identity deals with the history, culture, traditions and values that we recognize, respect and continue.

Our youth have been miseducated to believe in the American Dream of integration and assimilation. Many of our Elders gave up their dream of desegregation (making separate truly equal) and accepted integration as though it was their original goal or aim. Thus we have lost the antennae that enable us to recognize damaging, anti-Afrikan information. We have also, unfortunately, lost the desire to know ourselves. To our detriment, we were led to these conclusions by black organizations who were not Afrikancentered.

Being Afrikancentered will give us the understanding and "ammunition" to heal ourselves of this delusion.

Afrikan philosophy throughout the continent stresses that true development of the human being requires development of the physical, intellectual, emotional, psychological and spiritual selves. These values are equally important and must be developed equally. If only intellect is developed, the person becomes cold and abstract, if emotion is overdeveloped, the person becomes narcissistic and if the spiritual is overdeveloped out of proportion to the others, the person loses an anchor to the real world. As many Ausa "preachers" say, they become so heavenly bound that they are no earthly good.

Afrikancentered organizations provide a network for individuals that encourage them to support each other.

Afrikancentered organizations help preserve our heritage and help us to truly understand the devastating historicide that has been committed against us in the attempt to destroy our values, culture and traditions. They have a clear idea of Afrikan humanity and understand how Arabs and Europeans have attempted to destroy Afrikan humanity.

Afrikancentered organizations provide a family orientation that creates role modeling and positive peer pressure for children.

Afrikancentered organizations encourage, create and sustain camaraderie.

Afrikancentered organizations create avenues so that members can more easily "give back to the community".

Afrikancentered organizations give our people a vision and blueprint for a better tomorrow by helping us individually and collectively live up to our true potential.

Afrikancentered organizations perpetuate an Afrikan worldview which will ultimately save the world because of Afrikan respect for the Creator and the Creator's creations (nature and all life).

Afrikancentered organizations create and institute a proactive approach to the international Afrikan community rather than a reactive approach to

Eurocentric moves and to decide collectively on the proper set of goals in any circumstance.

Afrikancentered organizations foster academic and practical excellence.

Afrikancentered organizations participate in a profoundly important process that has provided the glue for Afrikan societies for thousands of years: the intergenerational transmission of knowledge. It provides for young people to not only know whose shoulders they stand on but gives them the opportunity to sit at the feet of the Elders.

Finally, in the King James version of the Christian Bible, there are verses that highlight what we are saying here: Hosea 4:6 states *"My people are destroyed for lack of knowledge: because thou hast rejected knowledge, I will also reject thee, that thou shalt be no priest to me: seeing thou hast forgotten the law of thy God, I will also forget thy children."* Understand that it says that it is not lack of faith or belief that will destroy God's people but a lack of knowledge of who they are as God's people.

To paraphrase our honored Ancestor, Dr. John Henrik Clarke, powerful people never teach powerless people how to be powerful. If we learn the oppressor's ways, we will come to believe that his way is the only way. Consequently, we will never know our way and will never know that our way may be better than the oppressor's way. We do know that the oppressor will never teach us how to be free or powerful.

Historian, Michael Bradley, a Euro-Canadian said in his book, Chosen People From the Caucasus":

"Afrikan Americans must forsake the white man's social structures, concepts of justice and yes, even his religion and return, as far as possible, to genuine Afrikan values and identity (in so far as these can be accurately recovered and reconstituted)."

If a race has no history, if it has no worthwhile tradition, it becomes a negligible factor in the thought of the world, and it stands in danger of being exterminated.

-Carter G. Woodson

HOW DO WE BECOME AFRIKAN-CENTERED?

Proverbs 3:31, in the Christian Bible says *"Envy not the oppressor, and choose none of his ways."* From this we can deduce that God does not want us to envy our oppressor because that would mean that we would want to imitate the oppressor. By doing this, we can never be truly free.

Since Afrikans first arrived in this country, there has been a debate between two groups of Ausa: those who wanted to integrate and assimilate with their European enslavers and oppressors and those who asserted their uniqueness and saw the need to join with other Afrikan peoples in the world towards a rebuilding and revitalization of Afrika. They saw the need to restore Afrika and Afrikan people (no matter where they are found) to their traditional greatness.

Our traditional greatness was to lead using Maat (truth, justice, balance, righteousness, harmony, divine order, and reciprocity) as our model. Most of the models being used at the present do not even take African people into account when being developed and implemented. That is one of the main reasons, why economic, political and social development has lagged or is nonexistent in Black communities. Afrikancenteredness, makes Afrikan people primary. Should not institutions take into account the culture and mores of the people to which they govern? Afrikan institutions would do so by their

J. Benton, T. Brice, B. Gallman, and D. Jackson

very natures, if done in an historically correct manner. They would not only take into account the higher needs of people, but also would manifest in a more natural state between spirit and reality. Current models of politics, laws, modes of production take into account only greed and self-aggrandizement, whereas Afrikan modes veer toward justice, balance and order. In other words, Afrikan models are much more humane.

Europe and European culture, cannot be used as a model of success because it is failing too many people, while oppressing so many others. Afrikancentered models tend to be more people friendly and for the bulk of human historical existence was the model most often used to govern self and others. The closer one finds itself to Afrikan models the more inclusive and beneficial to the community is the culture. As an example, worldwide universal medical care would be the norm rather than the insurance and business-based models of the United States, which is an ahistorical culture and one which is based upon wealth and privilege.

Whether we look at the situation from a micro point of view (Ausa people) or a macro point of view (Pan- Afrikan cohesiveness), we should remember that the concept of family in the Afrikan sense refers to what is called the extended family: a group of people who trace their beginnings from a common Ancestor. These people, as Gyekye attests, "are held together by a sense of obligation to one another" using communal values such as "solidarity, mutual helpfulness, interdependence, and concern for the well-being of every individual member of society".

In building institutions and starting organizations, we should ask how these organizations will benefit the Afrikan family. In other words, to paraphrase Dr. Anderson Thompson of the Kemetic Institute in Chicago, how will this organization do the greatest good for the greatest number of Afrikan people? This has been a continuing theme in this book, that we are obligated to "give back" to our community and our people. That is the Afrikan way.

Wherever we go in America, we are confronted with Eurocentric Western culture. The exceptions are when we go to a restaurant or festival representing another culture. Even then, that culture is frequently represented in a Eurocentric fashion.

Individually:

1. Write an autobiography, including a family tree and genealogical research. Find out information about each Ancestor (at least three facts). This is a great help towards fulfilling the dictate of our ancient Ancestors to "Know thyself".

2. Read and study Afrikan and Diasporan history from works written from our point of view. This is of profound importance.

3. If experience is the language of the spirit, then we must seek out Afrikancentered environments to experience, fortify and reinforce the Afrikan Worldview.

J. Benton, T. Brice, B. Gallman, and D. Jackson

4. Create study groups and collectively read, study and discuss works by our scholars and intellectuals.

5. Why Study Groups? As mentioned, there has been an intentional effort over the last 2000 years to not only strip us of all knowledge of who we are but also to remove the desire to know who we are. Our history has been kept from us and what little has gotten through to us has been changed. Much of the accomplishments of our Ancestors have been claimed by other people and taught to us as their history. After all, people who don't know their history make excellent slaves, regardless of the type of slavery or the time period (18th century or 21st century). Many Ausa have realized that they don't know as much about their history as they'd like to know or need to know. They are beginning to understand that not only have they been misled but that they are Afrikan people with a history that starts thousands of years before our kidnapping and enslavement in North and South America. Various aspects of our history have been well documented by scholars of Afrikan descent--who tell our story from our point of view. Studying with other people helps learning. Discussions can point out aspects of the material that you didn't consider. The repetition of good analysis helps in the retention of information.

Organizationally:

1. Include professional organizations, fraternities and sororities, and social organizations, when possible and hold them accountable to operating in the best interests of Ausa and all Afrikan people.

2. Assign the Areas of Human Activity (as suggested by Dr. Frances Cress Welsing) to organizations according to their specialty:

Economics. We should study economic systems of ancient and medieval Afrika (yes, there were Afrikan economic systems), as well as those used by early Ausa. Lessons learned should help improve the economic growth of Afrikan people. It should be seen that economics is not just about money but about the exchange of goods and services. Rotatory credit unions were prevalent throughout the continent of Afrika. These credit unions were collective savings for the purpose of purchasing real estate in urban settings. Members of an ethnic group pooled their funds to purchase property for the collective use of that group. This was also used to help a group member purchase and build a home in urban settings. Or, members contributed periodic deposits that, in turn, became available for interest free loans. There are multiple variations of this banking system . We see examples of this kind of system among early Ausa. In 1787, Richard Allen and Absalom Jones started one of the first formal social institutions for

Ausa, the Free African Society. This was a nondenominational mutual aid society designed to assist fugitive slaves and new migrants to Philadelphia. One objective of the Free African Society was to teach thrift and savings to build wealth among Ausa. Members were encouraged to deposit a certain amount of money per month to be used just in case "they, or their wives, widows, or children fell into poverty, provided that this necessity is not brought on them by their own imprudence". Members were expected to live a "sober and orderly life". In addition, there was an appointed committee of monitors to oversee the needs of Blacks in Philadelphia. These monitors conducted surveys of the needs of the community, and then provided those needs. The Free African Society provided access to funds, clothes, education, jobs, and religious services to those escaping slavery and to free blacks who were migrating to Philadelphia.

Education. Understand that excellence is the key and inspires students to always do their best to achieve excellence. The Ancient Afrikan educational system included apprenticeships. Students learned crafts, trades and professions from craftsmen and professionals through apprenticeships . There is a notion of "learning by doing" in a participatory observation. Because Afrika has a rich oral tradition, Afrikan schooling must infuse oral history as an interdisciplinary teaching tool. We must incorporate an Afrikan educational system. We must use our texts to teach our people about our people.

With this knowledge about ourselves, we will learn our true greatness and create expectations of excellence.

Entertainment. This might also be called "edutainment". Entertainment need not be mindless. It should create positive images of Afrikan people and foster positive self-image and self-worth. Ancient Afrikan entertainment required creativity. Music and dance were central. Musical instruments were created out of materials found in nature. Dances were used to teach life lessons (i.e. courtship, intergenerational communication). In our era of information accessibility, it is imperative that our entertainment system be shaped to provide education about ourselves, by ourselves. We cannot afford to waste another generation to mindless "entertainment".

Labor. Learning how collective work and responsibility can be operationalized in an Afrikan context. Ancient Afrikan labor tradition was generally owned in a collective manner. Property was shared by all members of the tribe, overseen by the elders. The land was worked collectively. The fruits of that labor were shared collectively. Labor was beneficial to the entire tribe. This is a difficult principle, particularly in the context of the capitalist system within which the Ausa finds themselves. This principle may be resurrected by our collective support for the well-being of our community (tribe). Our labor should benefit our community. This principle guides where we choose to labor, and how we choose to labor. The fruits of our labor should benefit our community (tribe).

Law. Ancient Afrikan law values truth and justice over judgment and retribution. This was a sophisticated conception and system of law. The principle of Ma'at is integral to Afrikan law traditions. Ma'at is a set of laws, grounded in justice and truth, intended to divert chaos. These 42 laws delineate ancient Afrikan concepts of truth, balance, order, law, morality, and justice. As Ausa, we must remind ourselves of the ancient Afrikan principle of Ma'at. We cannot adopt the definition of truth and justice of our oppressors. We cannot look to our oppressor to value truth and justice. We must use the principles of Ma'at as our guide, particularly as we address the needs of our community. We cannot afford to view each other with judgment and retribution.

Politics. Weighing the good of the people over the greed of the individual for power and the rewarding proven betrayal by our people. Ancient Afrikans conducted political decision making through consensus and free discussion. Consensus decision making was described by Kenneth Kaunda, the first President of Zambia in the following way:

In our original societies we operated by consensus. An issue was talked out in solemn conclave until such time as agreement can be achieved.

Furthermore Julius Nyerere, the first President of Tanzania, reminds us of this process:

The Quest for Self-Determination

In African society, the traditional method of conducting affairs is by free discussion.

This was done in a cooperative manner, not in a competitive way. The spirit of politics was intended to benefit the entire tribe. Ausa may struggle with this concept of collective politics that relies on consensus decision making. We must not look to the ways of our oppressor to develop policy strategies that benefit our community (tribe). We cannot use the socially constructed political parties of the oppressor to frame our discourse on the political needs of our community. We must rely on the collective needs of our community as a framework by which we develop political strategies. We cannot allow our oppressor to tell us who we should vote for, and how we should vote. We must develop our own system of politics.

Religion. As Ausa, it is mandatory that we know, study and understand the origins and history of religions as well as their dogma. We should know that Judaism came from ancient Afrikan Philosophy just like Christianity came from Judaism and Islam came from Christianity. We should know that the oldest images of Buddha in Asia have Afrikan features.

Sex. As Ausa, we must know the responsibilities of sexual behavior, procreation, responsibility and love. We must teach this to our children.

War. We should study Afrikan warriors such as Shaka of the Zulus, Hannibal, Queen Nzinga, the Candace queens of Kush as well as other Afrikans who excelled in war. We should create gun clubs and organize youth organizations to teach responsibility and discipline.

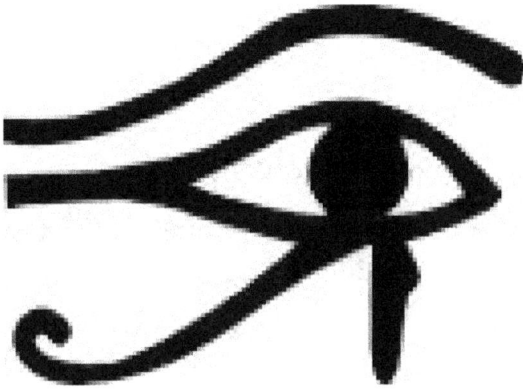

A Heru (All Seeing Eye)

Kujichagulia: Self-Determination
To define ourselves, name ourselves, create for
ourselves and speak for ourselves.

-Maulana Karenga

SELECTING AN AFRIKANCENTERED ORGANIZATION

Though most organizations, with a national or international scope did not start out with an Afrikan Centered agenda, those listed below are either evolving or have evolved into such a stance. Many of the organizations evolved from the Black Power movement of the sixties and seventies and through what is felt to be appropriate analysis came to the conclusion that the reclamation of African culture as the basis of healing was not only appropriate but also necessary. Afrikan people needed to be healed individually and collectively and did not need the good graces and approval of any other ethnic or racial group to do so. These groups and organizations realized that the human growth potential lies not in collaboration with oppressors but in moving toward the healing properties of self-determination.

There are many local movements that will not be listed here. But they are an important part of the trend toward Afrikan Centered development. The fear of recognizing these small but important actors, is the fear of leaving out or choosing between them, when they are all important.

Though not exhaustive, the following organizations are already trending toward Afrikancenterness in education, healing, or philosophy and are national or international in their scope:

J. Benton, T. Brice, B. Gallman, and D. Jackson

National Association of Black Social Workers
   www.nabsw.org

Association for the Study of African Classical
Civilizations
   www.ascac.org

Association of Black Psychologists
   www.abpsi.org

National Medical Association
   www.nmanet.org

National Association of Black Journalists
   www.nabj.org

Institute of the Black World 21st Century
   www.ibw21.org

Black Psychiatrists of America
   www.blackpsych.org

What these groups have in common is the tendency
to think and act Afrikan first. These groups are found to

be often at odds with their European Centered counterparts, yet have a separate agenda that is aimed at bettering Afrikan people with a focus upon culture and rituals of Afrikan culture being paramount. These organizations are unapologetic and are self-determining, often eschewing even financial assistance from outside groups.

These groups are adding Afrikan culture, cultural themes and information to its membership and greater Black community. They have become safe havens for Afrikan Centered thought, healing, evolving philosophy and modes of production. With open, rather than elitist membership, these groups offer membership regardless of title, social class or condition, while providing first class information, education, support and training.

These groups seek collaboration with like-minded Afrikan organizations and have joint projects in times of need, which may be a result of either manmade or natural disasters.

It is the sacred responsibility of Afrikancentered organizations to highlight the contradictions of our situation and then offer clear choices between that which is fostered under white supremacy and the better Afrikancentered solutions to today's problems. It is then that we can not only change the "table", but provide our people more than just hope, but a way out of our lives on the bottom.

J. Benton, T. Brice, B. Gallman, and D. Jackson

It will not be easy. There is a tremendous learning curve which involves not just paradigm changes, but world changing adjustments for individuals.

Duafe (Female Beauty)

To be African ...or not to be!

-Asa G. Hilliard,III

AFRIKANCENTERED VALUES AND PHILOSOPHIES

One of the main benefits of Africancentered philosophy and values is that they have been around for thousands of years and have been successful during that time. Too often today people try to solve perceived problems using variations of the same old remedies that always failed. Most of the time, these remedies are based upon European solutions. Our Ancestors told us that there are many approaches to solving problems and that they can all be useful in the lives of people. The first useful system was that of Maat. Maat is symbolically represented as a feminine principle and is the guiding force by which all things are governed. The ancients believed that adherence to these principles of Maat guaranteed a place in paradise.

Our Ancestors believed that value based education prepared the students to live a good, just, righteous and productive life. Material gain was not considered to be a goal of education. Other important value systems were the Declarations of Innocence and the Cardinal Virtues.

The principles of Maat were truth justice, righteousness, harmony, balance, order, propriety, and reciprocity. Maat though made up of simple words, is quite complex. The interesting thing about Maat is that she occurs whether she is wanted or not. Maat could be considered the natural order of things or Mother Nature.

J. Benton, T. Brice, B. Gallman, and D. Jackson

An even more complex system is that of the Cardinal Virtues. The Cardinal Virtues are based upon operationalizing Maat. The Cardinal Virtues are listed in order:

1. Control of thought.

2. Control of action.

3. Devotion of purpose.

4. Faith in the teacher's ability to teach the truth.

5. Faith in one's ability to know the truth.

6. Faith in one's ability to use the truth.

7. Freedom from resentment under persecution.

8. Freedom from resentment went wronged.

9. Ability to distinguish right from wrong.

10. Ability to distinguish the real from the unreal.

Then we come to the Declarations of Innocence, and Declarations of Virtue which are as old as Maat and the Cardinal Virtues. It was believed that if you lived by the principles of Maat and the 10 Cardinal Virtues, on judgment day the deceased would pass on into paradise. The declarations were 42 in number and were personal estimations of how one lived upon earth. Africans believed in personal responsibility and public good.

Finally, we must mention what we call the Afrikan Degrees of Knowledge. These have been described by Dr. Marimba Ani. They are descriptive of the degrees of maturity that it takes for individuals to navigate the world. They are:

Giri So   "Word from the front". This describes a simplistic mentality that interprets literally. It is sight without understanding.

Benne So   "Word from the side". This describes a thinking person who is able to interpret information and who is working towards establishing a point of view or perspective.

Bolo So   "Word from behind". This describes the ability of a person to penetrate to inner meaning and find the essenhis is insight.

So Dayi   "Clear word". This describes thought with understanding and seeing beyond the physical. This refers to 360 degree vision.

With these values and philosophies, African civilization was formed. These teachings were passed down for thousands of years and in most instances were diametrically opposed to European thought and philosophy. Culture is not only what you say but most importantly what you do. Doing Maat and living by the

J. Benton, T. Brice, B. Gallman, and D. Jackson

Cardinal Virtues yielded the type of human being that would be respected in all African cultures.

These values are difficult to live up to, especially when we consider the intentional damage that has been done to us in order to make us better slaves and for others to have access to the resources and riches of Afrika without having to pay for them.

Since Afrikans were brought to America by Europeans centuries ago, our humanity has too frequently been called into question (there is evidence that strongly suggests that Afrikans had been to the North American continent in the 800's B.C.E., more than 2000 years after Christopher Columbus got lost in the Caribbean). Even now, in the twenty-first century we are still perceived by most Americans as less than human. This perception has a long history and is so ingrained that many Americans of European descent have no empathy for the negative experiences that we suffer because of it. This has resulted in the systematized oppression and the slaughter of Ausa, especially young Ausa men. This makes the many positive values that we have attempted to inject into Western culture even more important. They are a testament to our humanity and speak to the fact that Afrikans have had ideals about moral obligation and social responsibility long before Europe had reached a point where they considered themselves to be civilized.

Afrikans are the prototype of what it means to be human, yet many of us have become "infected" with what many have called the Yurugu virus, imitating the worst of our oppressors. We act as if morals and ethics are foreign and excellence is "acting white" even though our Ancestors introduced these concepts to the world.

We must recover our collective memory, restore our place in the world and build upon what our Ancestors have accomplished. Our organizations have a duty and responsibility to be leaders, not only in our recovery, but leaders in the New World Order based in Maatian principles.

When you control a man's thinking you do not have to worry about his actions. You do not have to tell him not to stand here or go yonder. He will find his "proper place" and will stay in it. You do not need to send him to the back door. He will go without being told. In fact, if there is no back door, he will cut one for his special benefit. His education makes it necessary.

-Carter G. Woodson

RACISM, WHITE SUPREMACY AND WHITE PRIVILEGE

"They (that unfortunate race) had for more than a century before been regarded as beings of an infer or order and altogether unfit to associate with the white race, either in social or political relations, and so far unfit that they had no rights which the white man was bound to respect."

-Roger Taney (1857)
Last sentence of his opinion in Dred Scott V. Sandiford
("The Dred Scott Decision")

Those words expressed the prevailing attitude towards persons of Afrikan descent in the Nineteenth century and held sway until the mid-twentieth century.

At the dawning of the new century, the scholar-activist intellectual, W.E.B. DuBois (the first Ausa Harvard graduate) predicted that the major American problem of the twentieth century would be the color line. It appears that he gave Americans too much credit because race is still problematic in the twenty-first century.

It might be asked, "Why include a chapter on racism in a book about Afrikan Centered organizations?" If any of the reasons for AUSA organizations becoming Afrikancentered are related to racism, we must analyze and understand what racism is and isn't. Racism is alive, well and thriving in America. We must understand the effect that racism has on us as a people. Although there have been many examinations of racism (our bibliography is partial and deals with those evaluations that we feel to be particularly useful), we feel that the context is constructive. The necessity of Ausa organizations becoming Afrikancentered is made more urgent by the understanding of what racism and how it works. It is also made more urgent by the fact that the generation that we call "millenials" (those individuals born after 1980) may not have a realistic, historically-based view of racism. . While our ancestors fought for access to resources, this became misguided, resulting in what we recognize as integration. With integration comes assimilation. As a result, millennials tend to be more concerned with being like the oppressor, with little regard to the quality of the access to resources held by the oppressor.

Millennials have no memory of the American apartheid system of separate and unequal access. This generation has experienced relatively integrated schools, neighbor-hoods, workplaces, and social settings. They see Black faces on the television. They may have friends of diverse racial groups. Consequently, this generation has been lulled into believing that we are in a post-racial society. This generation is not aware of the oppressive structures in which they operate. While they have access to integrated schools, they are not aware that the quality of education is racially segregated. AUSA students tend to be less likely to participate in Advanced Placement classes offered in high schools. According to the 2013 ACT data, only 5% of AUSA students are prepared for college level work. And regardless of family income, AUSA students consistently score lower on the SAT than any other racial group. While AUSA can live in any neighborhood that they can afford, AUSA are more likely to pay more for that house than any other racial group.

AUSA students are less likely to understand that they are being hunted by the oppressor, whether the oppressor is state-sanctioned police or a scared White person. Our children have been lulled to sleep by the oppressor, and it is time for us to awaken them. This is the insidious nature of racism, White supremacy and privilege.

The concept of race is a social construct and not a biological reality as has been repeatedly demonstrated by DNA studies. Many Americans who "look black" and who identify as black may have more European genetic markers than Afrikan. It would not be impossible that a significant number of Americans who "look white" have predominately Afrikan genetic markers, especially considering the practice of light skinned blacks "passing" for white.

The terms "racism" and "white supremacy" are often used synonymously. However, in our context, white supremacy refers to the system under which we live. White supremacy is the current way of the world. Racism, which we will concentrate on here, is the major aspect of white supremacy but is not the only one. Age-ism, class-ism and sex-ism are also aspects of the system of white supremacy, especially if the Two Cradle Theory (which will be explained later) is taken seriously.

The term "racism" has meant different things to different people. It is interesting to watch people deny being racist after loudly, shrilly and publicly exhibiting racist behavior. While many of these vicious voices accept and bask in their racism, many others truly don't believe that they are racists. Are they self-deluded or are they victims of the same drama that has played out in America since its inception? Racism is as American as apple pie and permeates the air, water and dirt.

Definitions of Racism
Many have tried to define racism. While there is more than one definition, there are common currents that run through each definition. The concept of power is an important component in differentiating between racism and prejudice. The following are quotations from various scholars and scientists who have attempted to define racism:

"...(Racism is) the conscious and/or unconscious desire manifesting itself in whites to destroy, castrate and exploit black people both psychologically and physically due to inherent feelings of white superiority. In the context of racism in the English language, the definition implies that the language is designed either consciously and/or unconsciously to destroy and exploit black people psychologically by transmitting the racist culture through the language."

-David R. Burgest. The Racist Use of the English Language. *Black Scholar*, September 1973, pp. 37-45.

"His (Diop's) theory implies clearly that white racism was a result of early European nomadism and the ethnocentric-xenophobic mentality which resulted from it."

-Vulindlela Wobogo. Diop's Two Cradle Theory and the Origin of White Racism. *Black Books Bulletin*, Volume 4, Number 4, Winter, 1976, pp. 20-29, 72.

"Racism in the United States is a public health and mental health illness. It is a mental disease because it is delusional. That is, it is a false belief, born of morbidity, refractory to change when contrary evidence is presented concerning the innate inferiority of any person with dark skin color. Thus everyone in the country is inculcated with a barrage of sanctions which permit and encourage any white to have attitudes and behavior indicative of superiority over any black. Since everyone in involved in this delusion, then by definition it is a public health problem...In the classical mode of such illnesses, racism, besides affecting masses of population, also defies therapy on a one-to-one basis, produces chronic, sustained disability, and will cost large sums of money to eradicate...It is a contagious disease...it is a perceptual illness...the psychological hallmark of racism is the altogether too well known for whites to congratulate themselves before a black, concerning what marvelous 'progress' is being made...racism is a lethal disease."

-Chester Pierce: Offensive Mechanisms. *The Black Seventies* (5[31] 4) (Edited by Floyd B. Barbour, Porter Sargent Publications, pp. 265-282.

"Racism results from the transformation of race prejudice and/or ethnocentrism through the exercise of

J. Benton, T. Brice, B. Gallman, and D. Jackson

power against a racial group defined as inferior, by individuals and institutions with the intentional or unintentional support of the entire culture."

-James M. Jones (1991): Racism: A Cultural Analysis of the Problem. *Black Psychology* (Edited by Reginald L. Jones, Cobbs and Henry Publishers, Berkely, pp. 597-607.

"Fuller observed that, contrary to most present thinking, there is only one functioning racism in the known world- white supremacy. He challenges his readers to identify and then to demonstrate the superiority or functional supremacy of any of the world's "non-white" peoples over anyone. Concluding that since there is no operational supremacy of any "colored" people, Fuller reveals that the only valid operational definition of racism is white supremacy...it should be noted that, in the majority of instances, any neurotic drive for superiority usually is founded upon a deep and pervading sense of inadequacy and inferiority. Is it not true that white people represent in numerical terms a very small minority of the world's people? And more profoundly, is not "white" itself the very absence of any ability to produce color? I reason, then, that the quality of whiteness is indeed a genetic inadequacy or a relative genetic deficiency state, based upon the genetic inability to produce the skin pigments of melanin (which is responsible for all skin color). The vast majority of the world's people are not so afflicted, which suggests that color is normal for human beings and color absence is abnormal. Additionally, this state of color absence acts always as a genetic recessive to the dominant genetic factor of color production. Color always "annihilates"

68 | P a g e

(phenotypically and genetically speaking) the non-color, white. Black people possess the greatest color potential, with brown, red, and yellow peoples possessing lesser quantities, respectively. This is the genetic and psychological basis for The Cress Theory of Color-Confrontation and Racism (White Supremacy)."

-Welsing, Frances Cress, M.D. *The Isis Papers: The Keys to the Colors.* Third World Press, Chicago, 5³ ³ 5

"...in their relationship with the Black race, Europeans (whites) are psychopaths, and their behavior reflects an underlying biologically transmitted proclivity with roots deep in their evolutionary history. The psychopath is an individual who is constantly in conflict with other persons or groups. He is unable to experience guilt, is completely selfish and callous and has a total disregard for the rights of others."

-Wright, Bobby E., Ph.D. *The Psychopathic Racial Personality andOther Essays,* Third World Press, Chicago, 5³² 9

"Racism is a set of prejudicial attitudes and behaviors which are socially mediated by four components that serve as the mechanisms of white social dominance and discrimination. These components are the differential control of the power to enforce and influence decisions and outcomes; differential control of resources such as education, money and political influence; establishment of societal standards according to dominant white defini-tions, thus automatically marginalizing other group norms; and incorrect definition of problems such that

J. Benton, T. Brice, B. Gallman, and D. Jackson

perceptions and solutions are distorted, inappropriate, manipulatable, and dysfunctional."

-Byrd, W. Michael. and Linda Clayton, (1993): The African-American Cancer Crisis, Part II: A Prescription. Journal of Health Care for the Poor and Underserved 2 (2): 102-116

"Racism...is about an attitude or behavior that arises from a belief (i.e. a racist belief) that people can be differentiated from one another mainly or entirely on the basis of their ancestral lineage (referred to as races) often identified by some physical characteristics (e.g. skin colour, size of nose) but sometimes by behavioural characteristics (e.g. mannerisms), and that groups of people so categorized are to be treated as different in terms of their rights, capabilities and basic needs, with one or more groups being inferior to others."

-Fernando, Sumam (1984): Racism as a Cause of Depression. International Journal of Social Psychiatry 74 (5-2): 41-49, Spring

"From a medical and psychological standpoint both whites and blacks are deluded and victimized by white racism, for white racism is pro-white, anti-black paranoia...Whites need to heal themselves from unrealistic maladaptive narcissism and a sense of entitlement, from self-aggrandizement and denigration of blacks that prevents understanding, introjection and identification with blacks as humans of equal worth and has encouraged sadomasochistic (especially sadistic) relationships with blacks and with whites, thereby reinforcing the pregenital and immature elements in their personalities."

-Pinderhughes, Charles A., M.D.: The Origins Of Racism Int'l Journal of Psychiarty, 1969, 8(6) 934-941

Origins and History of Racism

The physical differences that define race were noted as long ago as humanity has been in existence. The differences were not given value, however so that the concepts of race and racism that we are dealing with in this work are relatively modern inventions.

There are many theories that deal with the origins of racism/white supremacy. We will briefly discuss a few of those theories.

The late Senegalese scholar, Dr. Cheikh Anta Diop, an Egyptologist, Cultural Anthropologist, Linguist and Nuclear physicist was an advocate of the monogenetic theory of man's origins. (31) He posited that the Africans who migrated North from Africa and got caught in Europe during the Wurm Interglacial Era (Ice Age) not only went through environmentally stimulated adaptive physical mutations resulting in what we now call a "white" or "Caucasoid" appearance but also experienced cultural and psychological adaptations that resulted in individual and societal aggressiveness, chauvinism, patriarchy, materialism and xenophobia.

According to Diop and one of his many disciples, Charles Finch, M.D., those mutated Africans, now called Europeans, encountered societies that had not needed to

J. Benton, T. Brice, B. Gallman, and D. Jackson

struggle against nature to survive. These people were peaceful and xenophilic and so the aggressiveness of the Europeans caused them to inferiorize and subjugate these peaceful people.

In another theory, Frances Cress Welsing, M.D., a psychiatrist, posits that racism is a subconscious survival mechanism of whites based on the recessive genetic patterns of many characteristics that associated with racial whiteness. She states that whiteness is a relative deficiency of melanin and that white people are a numerical minority worldwide who see people of color as a threat to their genetic survival since most of the characteristics that define blackness are genetically dominant and those that define whiteness are recessive. The result, she feels is hostility towards pigmented people and the imposition of white supremacy or domination. She actually defines racism as white genetic survival.

A commonly held idea is that racism as we know it today resulted from an attempt by Europeans to justify the institution of slavery through the use of pseudo-science.

Types of Racism

1. Individual Racism has also been called personally mediated racism, Dominative and Aversive Racism and Pre-Reflective/Post-Reflective Gut Racism. Individual racism includes emotional racial hatred that is acted out and justifies racial privileges. It also involves the creation of ideologies that posit the superi-

ority of some races and the inferiority of others. It rationalizes acts of racism. Individual racism is what most people think of when they hear the word, "Racism". This is also the "go to" definition when acknowledging other forms of racism. For instance, when the racist seeks to dismiss racism in all of its forms, the racist will defensively state, "I love all people. I have never used a derogatory name or mistreated a Black person". Individual racism is often believed to be the most incendiary form of racism. It is not.

2. Institutional Racism involves conscious and unconscious, even sometimes well-meaning manipulation of resources and institutions that impinge on rights and access of some racial groups. It is structural, having been codified into custom, practice and law. It involves inherited and definitional disadvantage. Institutional racism is structurally violent. It supports institutions, such as schools, law enforcement, social service institutions, and churches that are intended to be supportive of society's most vulnerable populations but are often violent against those populations. This results in racially disparate outcomes, such as low performing schools in poor (Black) communities, disproportionate involvement in the (in)justice system, underemployment, over-dependence on governmental assistance and interventions, and hyper-religiosity. Colloquially, this is what our more recent ancestors referred to when they would warn, "Honey, you have to work two

J. Benton, T. Brice, B. Gallman, and D. Jackson

or three times as hard to get what they (the oppressor) have".

3. Paternalistic Racism seeks to give whites the power to define what is good, right and needed for blacks . This is seen frequently in so-called liberal whites who may or may not be unconscious racists. This is often manifested in philanthropic efforts that claim to address the needs of vulnerable (read: Black) populations. However, those populations are never asked to identify those needs. There are many nonprofit organizations with missions steeped in paternalistic racism. They struggle to understand why their well-intentioned interventions are often not successful (as they deem them). Most telling, these organizations are perplexed when the target populations does not express gratitude for the organizations' paternalistic efforts.

4. Scientific Racism is pseudo-science that attempts to present racist ideology as scientific fact supported by research but in fact is distorted by a racist paradigm. The Western concept of objectivity in science is ignored. Eugenics is an example of scientific racism. Eugenics is the pseudoscientific social movement of the late nineteenth and early twentieth century that claimed to be able to improve the genetic features of human populations through selective breeding and sterilization. It was based on the idea that it was possible to distinguish between

superior and inferior populations. Eugenics was actually taught in some American medical schools and was practiced in the United States for many years before Hitler, inspired by the American Eugenicists created the inhuman pogroms of Nazi Germany. Although generally discredited, many Eugenic ideas are still in official existence.

5. Philosophical racism involves racist philosophies that may have originated centuries ago but are still clung to as if they were current. This is related both to scientific and institutional racism which, in some part, use this as a basis. A philosophical racist will use statistics, unfounded in evidence, and historical events, which are more folklore than fact, to support their racism. Philosophical racists rely on their reputations as authorities to advance their ideology.

6. Unconscious Racism is also called Color-Blind Racism. It involves treating people the same when in relevant respects they are different. It ignores the distinctive experiences and identities of blacks. When a color-blind approach is adopted to any social policy, whites are usually able to dominate because the common experiences are defined in terms which whites can more easily relate to than blacks. When someone says, "I don't see color", this is a blatant example of unconscious racism.

7. Internalized Racism is the acceptance of affected races regarding their own abilities and self-worth. It is manifested, for example, by blacks who side with obvious racists in impugning other blacks. In short, it is self-hatred and the hatred of others who look like them. Internalized racism is the basis for several mental disorders posited by the eminent experimental psychologist, Dr. Na'im Akbar:

The Alien Self Disorder "represents that group of individuals who behave contrary to their nature and their survival". They reject their inherent Afrikanness and blackness. They have materialistic and amoral preoccupations. It is very common in professional Ausa. We liken it to a variety of the Stockholm Syndrome.

The Anti-Self Disorder is similar to the Alien Self Disorder but also includes "overt and covert hostility towards the group of ones origin and by implications towards oneself". They identify with the oppressor, including the hostility towards their people (much like Uncle Ruckus on the cartoon *The Boondocks*).

The Self Destructive Disorders "represent the self-defeating attempts to survive in a society that systematically frustrates normal efforts for natural human growth". These disorders plus the low self-esteem associated with them give rise to the alternate economic systems associated with drug sales, pimping and prostitution, drug addiction (including alcohol) and mental illness.

Organic Disorders are "the result of physiological, neurological or biochemical malfunction...severely mentally defective, organic brain disorders and most of the commonly recognized forms of schizophrenia."

White Privilege

"The problem with a white culture of power is that it reinforces the racial hierarchy. As white people many of us expect to have things our way, the way we are most comfortable with. We may go through life complacent in our monoculturalism, not even aware of the limits of our perspectives, the gaps in our knowledge, the inadequacy of our understanding. We remain unaware of the superior status and opportunities we have simply because we're white...Having benefits and being part of the culture of power very often encourages a person to develop a sense of entitlement to special treatment. A sense of entitlement is the sense that you are owed certain rights, privileges, services, or material goods because of who you are... Racism distorts our sense of danger and safety. We are taught to live in fear of people of color. We are exploited economically by the upper class and unable to fight or even see this exploitation because we are taught to scapegoat people of color What is going on when white people claim reverse racism or claim to be victimized by people of color? Charges of reverse racism are usually part of a white strategy to deny white racism and to counterattack attempts to promote racial justice."

-Kivel, Paul. *Uprooting Racism: How White People Can Work For Racial Justice*. British Columbia, Canada, New Society publishers 2002, p.39, 42, 46, 61

J. Benton, T. Brice, B. Gallman, and D. Jackson

Of all the results of the Maafa, perhaps the ones most discussed and debated are the concepts of white **privilege and racism. Both of these philosophies arise** from the myth of white supremacy that was necessary to make it easier to kidnap, enslave, mistreat, and disorient Afrikan people, intentionally alienating them from their heritage and homeland and ultimately, themselves.

In America, whites and Blacks experience the world in completely different ways. The concepts of power, privilege and domination as exerted by whites are stark realities in Afrikan life in America.

There are different types of privilege that are not the same. Many are frequently used by those whites who deny white privilege to say that class privilege or sex privilege are more important. Some actually equate sexual orientation as more important than white privilege. It should be understood that individuals can be privileged in some ways but not in others. However, history and sheer numbers place white privilege at the pinnacle of privilege in America. It is also true that white privilege is very obvious to Afrikans in America but only to a few whites. As many have said, whites have the privilege of not knowing about their privilege. Unfortunately, Afrikans can do little or nothing about white privilege.

White privilege is the other side of racism and is the frequently subconscious feeling of entitlement and superiority that many whites, even some that are "well meaning", feel towards people who don't look like them. Many whites take this for granted. It enables them to take advantage of situations that favor them and ignore the fact that they are receiving special treatment not **afforded to people of color simply by being white in a world controlled by white people. White privilege enables white people to have to not work as hard to experience things that they take for granted.**

White privilege both feeds and results from racism. During the antebellum era, poor whites were mistreated and disrespected by wealthy whites. Frequently the only thing about their condition that they could feel good about was the fact that no matter how "bad off" they were, they were still "better than" the Ausa. Because wealthy land-owning whites saw this as a way of controlling their white subordinates, they exploited this feeling of false supremacy by actually giving poor whites slightly more privileges and respect than they gave Ausa. This situation continues today, especially in the way that many poor whites vote against their interests.

This privilege is manifested in many ways, including the attempt to universalize their experiences and opinions by saying that "all people do this" or feel like this, etc. Another way that whites see this privilege is their refusal (inability?) to understand what Afrikan Americans mean when they say that discrimination is still a problem. They seem not to be able to understand that white culture, opinions, and visions of reality are considered "normal" and other cultures, opinions, and visions are the "other" that lay outside of what is right and normal for them. Mere mention of "white privilege" frequently makes many white people very uncomfortable, much the same as many whites feel uncomfortable in situations in which they are not in the majority and are not the dominant person in situations.

This "cognitive dissonance" is at its most ridiculous when otherwise reasonably intelligent whites say that they oppose affirmative action because they believe in a "level playing field" where all people are equal, and no one has any advantages. This would be laughable if the results were not so tragic for Afrikan Americans.

Many, if not most white Americans are afraid to look objectively at the privilege that their whiteness gives them. In fact, many become very defensive and actually (ridiculously) project extra privileges onto Afrikan Americans. In admitting to the existence of white privilege, they admit to participating in the unfair advantage that they enjoy, and this is very uncomfortable to them.

Views of Racism

Racism is a mental illness caused by the delusion of white supremacy and is fed and supported in a symbiotic relationship by white privilege.
Racism is delusional. Racists hold to the belief of their own superiority despite all evidence to the contrary. Their evidence of their superiority is usually fabricated

information. They stack the deck against others and then blame these others for failing, using this failure as proof of inferiority. Because they control many information systems, they introduce and reinforce the idea of Black inferiority after taking away culture, which is the solid ground upon which and self-respecting people stand.

Racism is psychopathic. Psychopaths are in constant conflict with others. They are selfish, callous, unable to experience guilt and have a total disregard for the rights of others. They are violent. In photographic and written accounts of lynchings and other atrocities, women and children are often present. The present day equivalents of being hung, burned alive, or having body parts cut off while conscious are the beheadings, beatings, sodomizing in police stations, shootings, and being dragged behind trucks until the body fragments that we hear about in today's new, modern and "better" world.

Racism is an abnormal defense and adjustment mechanism against insecurities. These insecurities might be psychological or social. They might also be physical and related to the state of relative deficiency of melanin. This insecurity is manifested in the fact that many whites believe that Afrikan Americans are getting too many privileges since many Blacks are making material strides in this society. This insecurity borders on paranoia. It also may be an insecurity based on the relative genetic deficiency state of inability to produce melanin in significant amounts.

J. Benton, T. Brice, B. Gallman, and D. Jackson

Racism and white privilege are public health hazards because they are contagious delusions that affect masses of people.

Racism is not merely color prejudice, it is a sick, power-mediated ability to negatively influence the lives of others based on color, hair texture, and other physical features. It has profoundly affected the world for the worse and shows no sign of dying out. It is responsible for many of the troubles in today's world and is rapidly drawing the world to a cataclysmic end.

Bibliography and Suggested Reading

Akbar, Na'im. *Papers In African Psychology*. Tallahassee: Mind Productions & Associates, Inc., 2003

Better, Shirley. *Institutional Racism: A Primer on Theory and Strategies for Social Change*. Lanham: Rowman and Littlefield Publishers, 2008

Black, Isabella. Race and Unreason: Anti-Negro Opinion in Professional and Scientific Literature Since 1954. *Phylon: The Atlanta University Review of Race and Culture*, 36: 65-79, 1966

Bonilla-Silva, Eduardo. *Racism Without Racists. Color-Blind Racism and the Persistence of Racial Inequality in America*. New York: Rowman and Little0ield Publishers, Inc., 2014

Byrd, W. Michael and Clayton, Linda. *An American Health Dilemma: Volume One: A Medical History of African Americans and the Problem of Race: Beginnings to 1900*. NY: Routledge, 2000

Diop, Cheikh Anta. *The Cultural Unity of Black Africa*. Chicago: Third World Press, 1978

Finch, Charles S. Race and Human Origins. In: *Echoes of the Old Darkland: Themes From The African Eden*. Decatur, GA: Kenti, Inc. 1991

J. Benton, T. Brice, B. Gallman, and D. Jackson

Gallman, Burnett Kwadwo. *Sankofa University: Studying African-Centered History and Culture.* Columbia: Imhotep-The Drum, 2020

Haller, John S. Jr; *The Physician versus the Negro: Medical and Anthropological Concepts of Race in the Late Nineteenth Century. Bulletin of the History of Medicine 44: 154-167, 1970*

Jones, Camara Phyllis. *Levels of racism: A Theoretic Framework and a Gardener's Tale. American Journal of Public Health, 2000; 90: 1212-1215*

Jones, James. *Prejudice and Racism. New York: McGraw Hill, 1972*

Kovel, Joel; *White Racism: A Psycho-History. NY: Vintage Books, 1972*

Krieger, Nancy; *Shades of Difference: Theoretical Underpinnings of the Medical Controversy on Black/ White Differences in the United States, 1830-1870. International Journal of Health Services, 17: 259-278, 1987*

Valls, Andrew (Editor); *Race and Racism in Modern Philosophy. Ithica: Cornell University Press, 6449*

Akofena (Courage)

J. Benton, T. Brice, B. Gallman, and D. Jackson

"The hard fact is that most of what we now call world history is only the history of the first and second rise of Europe...more than five thousand years had unfolded before what was to become Europe was a political factor in world affairs."

-John Henrik Clarke

HOW WOULD AN AFRIKANCENTERED WORLD LOOK?

We have discussed Afrikancentered culture. We have outlined Afrikan Axiology, Cosmology, Epistemology, Aesthetics, Ideology, Ontology, Ethos, Logic, Pedagogy, Process and Methodology. We have described Maat, which our Kemetic Ancestors tried to live by. Kemet was by no means perfect but reached a point that was closer to perfection scientifically, ethically and spiritually, that the world has ever seen. That near perfection was due to the efforts by the people to live up to the ideals of Maat (truth, justice, righteousness, harmony, balance, order and reciprocity). What we propose to do now is to describe what we feel that an Afrikan world would look like. Some may say that Afrikans ruled the world for much of its history and didn't do much with it. However, our study of history and culture informs us that Afrika was more advanced materially, intellectually, culturally and spiritually than the rest of the world for the overwhelming majority of that period. As we've described, it took military defeat confounded by error in judgments (welcoming and trusting visitors who didn't deserve either and who meant us no good) to start us on the dark road that we currently find ourselves on. It should be emphasized that the following is a view of the end product not the methodology of achieving it. That is a topic for another time. Every person has a dream for her/his future at one time or another. This is our dream.

An Afrikancentered world would be peaceful, harmonious and ordered. Each individual within this society would simultaneously be allowed to define themselves and what they want to be but within the **wide boundaries set by the societal norms. This is not to say that no one would be allowed to "think outside the box" but any thoughts or actions that threatened the society would be discouraged. However, for those who insisted on pursuing potentially damaging actions, a place would be set aside for them to do this and if a way of fitting it into society without damaging the order could be found, they would be gradually integrated back into society.**

At this juncture, we have the advantage of 20-20 hindsight if we would only open our eyes. We should be able to see the mistakes that our ancient and recent Ancestors made.

We will describe our vision of an Afrikan centered world using the Nine Areas of Human Activity, discussed by Dr. Frances Cress Welsing as the outline.

<u>Economics.</u> Economics is the study and practice of making choices in regard to how all resources are used and allocated. By its very nature, economics is always in a state of flux. The two major systems that have dominated the last one hundred fifty years have been either capitalism in its various forms or communism. Though somewhat different, both communism and capitalism require a class system based upon a constant tension between the upper and lower classes. With capitalism, the deck is stacked against the lower and middle classes while communism seeks to maintain a

never-ending struggle between the classes. An Afrikancentered world would mean the destruction of capitalism and communism as we know them.

The Afrikan mode of production or economic system seeks an ideal of no class distinctions but depends on the cultural base of developing relationships. In an Afrikancentered world, business economic development and distribution of wealth reinforces the notion of relationship and is built from the bottom up as opposed to top down as in capitalism. An Afrikan business would be based upon the collective need to act. For example, the Afrikan mode of production in the area of supplying clean sheets and towels to a hospital would mean that those individuals who do the laundry would band together to do the collective work but would hire someone to negotiate their contract with the hospital. They would hire another group to pick up and distribute the dirty towels and sheets. These laundry-doing individuals would share the profits, select the negotiator and choose all the components needed to enhance the business. They would also select hierarchy (supervisors if needed) who report to the laundry-doing individuals who would pay competitive salaries to all involved. As the business prospers, all would prosper. This is but one example, but banking, home ownership, the purchase of and making of commodities would be similarly constituted. Our current system, which may be on its last leg only assures financial gain to those at the top, while the middle keeps the bottom in check and satisfied with low wages.

In an Afrikancentered world, everyone would be on essentially the same economic level, working for the community. Those who provided the most would benefit in respect and stature, not material wealth, although every productive member of the society would be deemed worthy of respect. This would be a world governed by reciprocity.

Education. An Afrikancentered education would include the necessities (reading, writing, mathematics) taught at earlier ages. Algebra, Trigonometry and Geometry, etc. would be subjects for primary and elementary aged students. They would include the truthful history of their origins and would be taught with a truthful and accurate cultural grounding. Social studies would be accurate, and the history of the world would be taught from the perspective of Afrikan people but would truthfully include the histories of other people. The emphasis would be placed on maximal achievement rather than minimum standards. Students would be taught the great value of all life.

Entertainment. Afrikan people are very creative and the forms of entertainment (music, poetry, comedy, drama, prose [fiction and non-fiction]) would not change. What would change would be the way that topics would be presented, and the high value placed on them. Afrikan people would always be portrayed as the heroes and she-roes of every genre. The exploitation of violence, crass sexuality and mindlessness would not be allowed. Athletics would be valued but not glorified.

Entertainment (including athletic spectacles) would no longer be one of the opiates of the masses.

Labor. Labor in an Afrikancentered world would hold a highly respected place regardless of what that labor may be. Work would be viewed as making the community **pleasant and safe while providing a modicum of safety to all. All business would emanate from the ranks and from the collective actions of the labor force. Salaries would therefore be based upon equity and abilities needed by the group. In other words, salaries would be based on what the group is willing to pay and the value placed on the service, as opposed to social status in the rank ordering of the benefits of one profession over another. All work would be viewed as essential to the development, maintenance and growth of the economy in the community. Labor, like its overarching system, economics, would be based upon developing and enhancing relationships as opposed to the profit motive.**

Law. Ideally, in a Maatian world, there would be no need for law enforcement and lawyers, etc. however we are human and prone to human frailties. There would be councils of Elders that would judge disputes and pronounce decisions. The Elders would be impartial and fair. Their decisions would be accepted as final. If punishment of any kind was felt to be warranted, the worst punishments would be ostracization and/or banishment from the community. This would be a terrible fate because of the closeness of the sense of community that would be present.

<u>Politics.</u> Although all human relationships are political, to be accused of being a politician would be frowned upon. Politics depends upon compromise. Too often, politicians today compromise principles that they know to be correct for what they see as the "greater good". In a Maatian world, right and good are not compromised. In a Maatian world, ideally, there would be no need for compromise. However, if disagreements arose, the impartial Council of Elders would be the final authority.

<u>Religion.</u> One's belief system is highly personal and should be respected by all others. It is recognized that a religion is a human way of objectifying a philosophy. Or, to paraphrase Dr. Yosef ben-Jochannan, religion is the deification of a culture. In an Afrikancentered world, there would be no ranking of religions and no imperialistic actions to convince others to believe as you believe. The basic tenet of life would be to be the best person possible, to glorify the Creator and honor the Ancestors. The style or manner that you did these things would be a matter of personal preference.

<u>Sex.</u> The difference between the sexes would be recognized and respected, however, there would be no division of labor based on sex. Anyone who could adequately perform any duty would be allowed to perform that duty. The relationship between the sexes would be based on mutual respect. Sexual intimacy would not be trivialized, sensationalized and minimized as just a physical function that felt good. It would be seen

as a sacred act bonding the spiritual and intellectual relationship of the partners as well as the physical.

<u>War.</u> Again, ideally, there would be no war in a Maatian world. However, all nations must have a way of defending their way of life from those who would destroy them.

J. Benton, T. Brice, B. Gallman, and D. Jackson

Sesa Wo Suban
(Change or Transform Your Character)

SUMMARY AND DISCUSSION

One question that has been asked frequently is: What does it mean to be Afrikancentered? There are many answers to that question. Some are:

1. Being Afrikancentered is a transformational process that changes how one sees the world and engages in the political, social and economic realities of living in this world. This process is restorative in that it will begin the healing process and rebuild that which has been ruined.

2. Being Afrikancentered gives us clarity in understanding the complicated nature of our plight and the ongoing world-wide struggle wherever Afrikan people are found.

3. Being Afrikancentered is to understand that the Liberation Movement of which we speak started when the very first Afrikan was kidnapped and enslaved by the Arabs as well as the Europeans (the East Afrikan Arab slave trade flourished for approximately 700 years before the European slave trade). We must understand the battles and the suffering of our Ancestors as they fought against this pernicious institution.

4. To be Afrikancentered is to know that Afrikans were brought to America, not slaves.

5. To be Afrikancentered is to accept the values that have been passed down to us from our ancient Afrikan Ancestors.

Gye Nyame (God is Supreme)

J. Benton, T. Brice, B. Gallman, and D. Jackson

QUESTIONS FOR CONSIDERATION AND DISCUSSION

1. What do you think that our Ausa Ancestors talked about after the end of formal slavery?

2. Do we need Eurocentric institutions in order to be successful?

3. Do you really think that Ausa and other people of Afrikan origin have been brainwashed to any extent?

4. What does Afrikancentered mean from your perspective?

5. What do you owe those Ausa who fought and frequently died in order to make things better for you and future generations?

REFERENCES AND SUGGESTED READINGS

Ani, Marimba. Yurugu: *An African-Centered Critique of European Cultural Thought and Behavior.* Trenton: Africa World Press, 1994.

Anonymous (2008). Why Family Income Differences Don't Explain the Racial Gap in SAT Scores The Journal of Blacks in Higher Education (62), 10-12

Asante, Molefi Kete and Abu S. Abarry (Editors). *African Intellectual Heritage: A Book of Sources.* Philadelphia: Temple University Press, 1996.

Baradat, Leon P. *Political Ideologies: Their Origins and Impact.* Upper Saddle River, New Jersey: Pearson Prentice Hall, 2009.

Benton, Joe, Derrick Jackson, Burnett Gallman. *Project: Sankofa: A Rites of Passage Program: Philosophy, Theory & Overview.* Columbia: Our Community Organization, 5[332].

Better, Shirley. *Institutional Racism: A Primer On Theory And Strategies for Social Change.* New York: Rowman and Littlefield Publishers, Inc. 2008.

Bonilla-Silva, Eduardo. *Racism Without Racists: Color-Blind Racism and the Persistence of Racial Inequality in America.* New York: Rowman and Littlefield Publishers, Inc., 2014.

Browder, Anthony T. *Exploding the Myths, Volume 7: Nile Valley Contributions to Civilization*. Washington, DC: The Institute of Karmic Guidance. 1992.

Browder, Anthony T. *Survival Strategies for Africans In America: 13 Steps To Freedom*. Washington, DC: The Institute of Karmic Guidance, 1996.

Browder, Anthony T. *From the Browder File: 88 Essays on the African American Experience*. Washington, DC: The Institute of Karmic Guidance, 2000.

Burrell, Tom. *Brainwashed: Challenging the Myth of Black Inferiority*. New York City: Smiley Books, 6454.

Carruthers, Jacob H. *Intellectual Warfare*. Chicago: Third World Press, 1999.

Chinweizu. *Decolonising the African Mind*. Lagos: Pero Press, 1987.

Clarke, John Henrik. *Who Betrayed The African World Revolution? And Other Speeches*. Chicago: Third World Press, 1995.

Ezekiel Dixon-Roman, Howard Everson, & John McArdle (2013). Race, Poverty and SAT Scores: Modeling the Influences of Family Income on Black and White High School Students' SAT Performance Teachers College Record, 115 (4), 1-33

Finch, Charles S. *Echoes of the Old Darkland: Themes From the Africa Eden*. Decatur, GA: Khenti, Inc, 5³³ 5.

Gallman, Burnett W. *The Shoulders We Stand On.* (Unpublished Manuscript), 1999.

Gallman, Burnett Kwadwo, Marimba Ani and Larry Obadele Williams (Editors). *To Be Afrikan: Essays by Afrikans in the Process of Sankofa: Returning to our Source of Power. Volume 1.* Atlanta: M.A.A.T., Inc., 6447.

Gallman, Burnett Kwadwo. *Reparations: Quick and Concise Considerations.* (Unpublished Manuscript), 2003.

Gallman, Burnett Kwadwo. *The Black Pages: To Be Afrikan.* (Unpublished Manuscript), 2005.

Gyekye, Kwame. *African Cultural Values: An Introduction.* Philadelphia: Sankofa Publishing Company, 1996.

Hilliard, Asa G. III. *Sba: The Reawakening of the African Mind.* Gainesville, FL: Makare Publishing Co., 5331.

Hilliard, Asa G III. *African Power: Af6irming African Indigenous Socialization in the Face of the Culture Wars.* Gainesville, FL: Makare Publishing Co. 2002.

Jackson, John G. *Introduction to Black Civilizations.* Secausus, NJ: The Citadel Press, 1970.

Kambon, Kobi Kazembe Kalongi. *Cultural Misorientation: The Greatest Threat to the Survival of the Black Race in the 21st Century.* Tallahassee, FL: Nubian Nations Publications, 2003.

J. Benton, T. Brice, B. Gallman, and D. Jackson

Lemelle, Sid. *Pan-Africanism for Beginners.* New York: Writers and Reading Publishers, Inc. 1992.
Madhubuti, Haki R. *Enemies: The Clash of Races.* Chicago: Third World Press, 1978.

Nobles, Wade W.: *African Psychology: Toward Its Reclamation, Reascension and Revitalization.* Oakland, CA: A Black Family Institute Publication. 1986.
Stuckey, Sterling. *Slave Culture: Nationalist Theory and the Foundations of Black America.* New York: Oxford University Press, 1987.

Thiong'o, Ngugi wa. *Something Torn and New: An African Renaissance.* New York: Basic Civitas Books, A Member of the Perseus Books Group, 2009.

Welsing, Frances Cress. *The Isis Papers: The Keys to the Colors.* Washington, DC: C.W. Publishing, 5[33] 5.

Williams, Chancellor. *The Destruction of Black Civilization: Great Issues of a Race From 4500 B.C. to 2000 A.D.* Chicago: Third World Press, 1976.

Willis, W. Bruce. *The Adinkra Dictionary: A Visual Primer on The Language of Adinkra.* Washington, DC: The Pyramid Complex, 1998.

Wilson, Amos N. *Blueprint For Black Power: A Moral, Political and Economic Imperative for the Twenty-First Century.* New York: Afrika World InfoSystems, 5[332].

Wilson, Amos N. *The Falsifcation of Afrikan Consciousness: Eurocentric History, Psychiatry and the Politics of White Supremacy.* New York: Afrika World InfoSystems, 5³ ³ 7.

Young, Iris Marion. *Justice and the Politics of Difference.* Princeton, NJ: Princeton University Press. 1990.

ABOUT THE AUTHORS

Joe Benton has conceptualized, planned, organized and implemented human service programs for more than 40 years. Born and reared in Seattle, Washington, he has earned a B.A. degree from Benedict College in Columbia, SC, an M.S.W. from the University of Washington in Seattle, WA and has done further study at the Wharton School of Business at the University of Pennsylvania and did intensive study of history at the University of Bristol in Bristol, England. Joe writes, has taught psychology, history and sociology at the Columbia Junior College (now South University). More than 300 troubled boys and girls have graduated from Joe's Afrikancentered manhood and womanhood programs at St. Luke's Center and elementary and middle schools in the Columbia, SC area. Joe was the 11th National President of the National Association of Black Social Workers and served for five years as the Special Assistant to the Bishop of the 7th Episcopal District of the AME Church. He is married and the father of two and takes great pride in his three grandchildren.

Burnett Kwadwo Gallman is a native of Hartsville, SC and a graduate of Benedict College, Columbia, SC and Hahnemann Medical College and Hospital (now Drexel University) in Philadelphia, PA. He practices Gastroenterology in Columbia and is an employee of the WJB Dorn Veteran's Administration Hospital in Columbia. He serves on the National Board of the Association for the Study of Classical African Civilizations and as Advisor to the immediate past President of NABSW.

He has participated in the development of Rites of Passage programs and created a shadowing program for young people interested in healthcare careers. He has written papers and books and lectured to community organizations, religious organizations, educational organizations and penal institutions throughout the USA and Ghana on Afrikancentered Rites of Passage, the importance of symbols to Afrikan people, homosexuality, environmental racism, Black Greek letter organizations, the importance of names, ancient Egypt, mental slavery of Afrikan people and various topic in Afrikan and Diasporan (especially Ausa) History. He is married and is the father of one daughter.

Dr. Tanya Smith-Brice is Vice President of Education at the Council on Social Work Education in Alexandria, VA. Previously, she has served as Dean of the College of Professional Studies at Bowie State University in Bowie, MD and Dean of the School of (Education) Health and Human Services at Benedict College in Columbia, SC. She has served on the faculties of the University of South Carolina, Abilene Christian University (Abilene, TX), and Baylor University (Waco, TX). Her research centers on addressing issues of structural violence specifically as it relates to the impact of those structures on African American people. Her publications focus on the development of the social welfare system by African American women for African American children and documents structural barriers to African American families. She provides consultation to community organizations, religious institutions, and educational institutions on the impact of their policies on African American families. She has taught and lectured all over the USA, as well as in the countries of Ghana, Sweden, Uganda, Colombia and the Republic of Moldova. Dr. Brice earned a PhD from the University of North Carolina at Chapel Hill, an MSW from the University of South Carolina, and a BSW from South Carolina State University.

Baba Derrick Jackson is a native of Harlem, NY and is an ordained priest who completed his indoctrination into the Priesthood with a special concentration on Afrikan and Ausa cultural and religious institutions. He is the Senior Pastor of KRST Universal Temple, an Afrikan-centered religious institution that uses ancient wisdom texts featuring the Gospel According to Ancient Kemet as its foundation. He completed the course of study at the Cooper-Lewter Institute for study, application and advancement of Soul Therapy and its four aspects: Biological-Psychological-Sociological and Spiritual Development. He has served as lecturer and consultant on Classical Afrikan History and Rites of Passage Programs. He has worked extensively with "at-risk" youth throughout South Carolina, assisting with Rites of Passage programs. He assisted in the development of the award winning St. Luke Rites of Passage program which has graduated more than 300 trainees since 1989. He is married and the father of one daughter.

"We must work as if it's impossible to fail."

-Ashanti Proverb

www.ingramcontent.com/pod-product-compliance
Lightning Source LLC
Chambersburg PA
CBHW072201270326
41930CB00011B/2505